RICHARD PRICE was born   ined as
a journalist at Napier Coll   at the
University of Strathclyde,   ationist
group of poets, he was a f _____ them,
Gairfish and *Southfields*. He is also the co-founder of Vennel Press, the
imprint which brought earlier Informationist collections to a wider audience.
He is Head of Modern British Collections at the British Library, London.

RICHARD PRICE

Lucky Day

CARCANET

Acknowledgements

I am especially grateful to the editors who first published earlier versions of several sequences and individual poems collected here in fine and small press editions: to Nicole Presentey and Chan Ky-Yut of Lyric Press (*A Twenty-Piece Puzzle*), to the late Ian Robinson of Oasis Books (*Scape*), to Ian and Sally King of Diehard Poetry (*Frosted, Melted* and *Perfume & Petrol Fumes*), and to Duncan Glen of Akros (*Marks & Sparks* and *Hand Held*). 'Farewell remembering a goodbye' first appeared in *César Vallejo: Translations, Transformations, Tributes*, edited by Stephen Watts and myself (Southfields Press), and 'Air miles' in *Onsets*, edited by Nate Dorward (The Gig).

Other poems collected here were first published in *Cul-De-Qui*, *Morning Star Folios*, *The Eildon Tree*, *Poetry Scotland*, *Poetry Review*, and *PN Review*.

'A Spelthorne Bird List' was first premiered at the Troubadour Coffee House, Earls Court, in January 1998.

'the frame' is dedicated to the artist Dorothy Stirling whose beautiful paintings so intrigue and delight me, and who has kindly allowed the reproduction of 'Taking Flight' for the cover of this collection.

Peter, David, Donny and Raymond – my thanks as ever.

First published in Great Britain in 2005 by
Carcanet Press Limited
Alliance House
Cross Street
Manchester M2 7AQ
Copyright © Richard Price 2005

The publisher acknowledges financial assistance from Arts Council England

Typeset by XL Publishing Services, Tiverton
Printed and bound in England by SRP Ltd, Exeter

Contents

SCAPE

A SPELTHORNE BIRD LIST

LICK AND STICK

OFFICES

MARKS & SPARKS

HAND HELD

A NEWS

ALL LIGHT

Scape

*

All the days back up in the flooded valley.
The 'kids' villages' are gone, and St John's Wort
in flickers of yellow. Glands taken for wounds.

Pick me up. The dam's this forehead,
all fatigue and no foundation.
Shaky electricity. Sip, sip, sip,

and please, from a minute's infusion
cheer the hours up. Like, or love?
Our small city is lit by water.

*

They were your letters yesterday
floating down on a depth of years.

It was swan upping
but no livery company
could clip a tag
round your defiant cygnets.

One fledgling proclamation –
'love, I think' –
from your Pilot Fineline
would still outrank

the Royal Assent,
shoplifter,
and you fly
with a life warrant, now.

Dual sculls

The rowers swear their thrusting paintbrushes' tensioned craft
– muscular infant counting – up now to the first, the first
of all bridges, to be nothing for the moment beyond that survival.

(An engine drags tens of ramped cars on top of them,
all backwards, with a clatter and the bargain cutlery
of metallic-finish glints.)

*

Supper will keep: chicken periods
nested with your comb, your compact phone;
your electronic urgentiser.

You're smudging your watch on a semi-fast,
snubbed, you say, by freight.
There's a crash text in cream on red.

In the event of a serving suggestion
break the glass with an egg.

*

the broad bellies of the working barges,
working barges (retired) – long, broad, barges

her pale belly, sun-shy, faintly striped –
'children do stretch you' –

to be proud of your own skin –
a case of back then –

repairs and conversions,
sanded 'thoughs' and 'seeings-as'

the river constricted, hastened
by grandeur

(side-by-side
like two old barges)

Pylons

Pylons queue like dieted brides
just in charge of their lives,
hauling their hems
        high up off the earth.

On their happiest day
who throws the bouquet
        is lightning.

the frame

is integral

*

a brass trig point
a worked moor

*

a seine net
casting the hill

*

(this overlaps to frame, includes)

the sky overlaps to frame, includes

*

triangulated
by the peak

we are
our bearings

at home
in our surroundings

*

Rare calm on the rattled moor.
The breeze

holds its breath.

The installation,
the stilled lawn of concept blooms –

giant, whited,
hardly petalled –

idles.

She loves me /
she loves me not.

Three oasthouses

Two nuns in chatter,

        but a further –

looking away.

        A secret is not,
        couldn't

a secret cannot be safe.

Yes a uniform,
rich cream-and-brown,
the taut cowl.

Are nuns and oasthouses
pitchers?

'Pictures.'

        A secret, just
        contained.

'The accident cash
      is in the jug.'

– domestic space –

'Why are you always
      ganging up on me?'

the secret   the secret   the secret

'I *had* to leave
      you and everywhere.'

(green–yellow cones,
their resinous glands:
hops)

drying up.

                                             bitter /
                                             taste that /
                                             quite some flavour.

A world without earth

High ground. A wasp imposter, caught,
in a sundew.

Something almost paper, all twitch
in something almost flesh.

Yellows and dark browns. Mouthy reds.
A barely green, a green that's known

a world without earth.

You specialise, and it's survival.
A vocal windpipe and the gamble,

the gamble is you'll choke.
Luck is determination

in a look back.

You're an ape, planning to sing.
'I'll just keep talking...?' –

a friend, against the coma.
Crackable fingers can draw.

Twitch, flesh, earth.

(Intricate wasp imposter,
intricate sundew.)

Net results

A trawler, a converted trawler, slows,
adjusts, backs back towards its boasting wake.
Hung like blubber, five fenders take the blows.

The boat has docked, has stopped, make no mistake,
for good. The lamp that lights must settle down
for homely duty, for land-tied nudge and shake.

The ocean's over. Fish now board alone,
with oats, in surreptitious poly bags.
Time drags, in houseboats. Customs never phone.

Dogger

fish

folk and fish

dogs and folk and fish

floods and dogs and folk and fish

floods and folk

dogfish

Motorcruisers –

croupiers' caps in reinforced ice-cream, in
tennis shorts, in
cakebox and flipflops –
in fours and fives, a lock's worth,
the circus white horses / cattle, weighty-afloat,
the tall bleached shires with cold blue vizors –
the past master shotputters, the mooer-and-shaker, wagering stockbrokers,
the flecked-wedge white horses,
bovine, lining up
in the dainty tonnage contest
(sleeps two times two, plus two).

In the acting captain's jargon
did I mention the glint of stauntion?,
how the klaxons bugle dense champagne –
or sparkling wine at least –
how the secret cleats
lie low, half ashamed
of the galleon carton?

The tenders on tenterhooks expect
the dregs (fluffed up), the float-trot
to worry the weed-wisp water,
to swill the willow-shadowed shallows,
to spread that turbo spit.

The lotion-going powerboats
gargle past apologetic patios,
spinnaker swans and grasping coot.
Their engines churn and spurt, slosh
the coughs of brilliant white froth.

'Kids, keep to the path.'

Candid,
above, ahead,
the motorway bridge.

Better trees

Trees are the roots of better trees
that thrive beneath the beaten filament,
stabilised – by deep breezes.

Stop cremations.
Graves are airlocks and provide.

the white horse

the Horse says scrub
ensure the year with aches and jokes
to marry her two months after
it's said says to do that

the colour white dug in
deeper than a surface
you could not
disremember the slaughter

it can't contain meaning
close up
that's when we do together
singing working

scour the year the next appears

try to flee
the Horse you'll see

you/you'll variant
rider absent

The organised forest

'Scarper!' is polite by half – you're thirty years younger,
arms full of outdated diction, scrumping apples in a clearing,
skew-whiff on a damp stack, placebo sacred –
almost compost – of popular classics.

'Love letters and local news bear fruit.'

You're a version, tom-boy, from a translator
who's a shaky translation himself –

'You just like the sound
of your own vocative,
but it's no good "you" having the last word.'

Apples don't grow on trees in your latest testimony:
they ooze as paste in an envelope of fat.
You're a justified shoplifter – the food is fast
but there are so many repeats.

'Head Office dropped all charges. They're afraid –
of their own ingredients.'

Scarper. As you exit the organised forest
there should be swearing for realism,
for a cutting edge
(it must be a thrill to be real,
to threaten with something sharp),
but let's not fight about register –
I find your joke about 'Shameless Honey' unfair
but it leaves a not unpleasant taste in the mouth.

I have the courage of my lack of convictions,
so let the old light in the walled orchard
set the dappled tone: the scent of cinnamon and Bramleys,
my mother's special, guides me sometimes,
but I think of you as a child as well,
head of the family.

Round about then, you were turning
mushy peas out of a tin – some apples –
but you didn't glean the alphabet from shaped spaghetti.
I can't… get carried away with yourself,
I've never been a lookout.

'Scarper!' wishes me back into your gang –
I know now you always act alone.
Really, I'm a lucky incomer's son
yelling for the sake of sound:

'Come back, I only want
to talk to you!'

For December

The broken song
is off its crutches.

The wood is lit –
and the fire catches.

A Spelthorne Bird List

The name Spelthorne is a Saxon word meaning 'Speech Thorn Tree'.
John Mills, *A Guide to the Industrial History of Spelthorne*

Hedge Sparrows

You don't see many hedges these days, and the hedges you do see they're not that thorny, it's a shame, and when I say a hedge I'm not talking about a row of twigs between two lines of rusty barbed wire, or more likely just a big prairie where there were whole cities of hedges not fifty years ago, a big desert more like, and I mean thick hedges, with trees nearby for a bit of shade and a field not a road not too far off so you can nip out for an insect or two when you or the youngsters feel like a snack, a whole hedgerow system, as it says in the book, and seven out of ten sparrows say the same, and that's an underestimate, we want a place you can feel safe in again, we're social animals, we want our social life back, and the sooner the better, because in a good hedge you can always talk things over, make decisions, have a laugh if you want to, sing, even with a voice like mine!

Coot

The coot was a pint of stout. It slipped out from The Ferry during a fight. Mathematically white, it was plunged by its beak in mathematical black. To uppity swans it does not signify. The same goes for Joe Duck.

Mandarin Duck

The box of a frozen-food tiramisu misfolded into a crumple. Looking for its reading glasses. Feral in Surrey.

Great Crested Grebe

My favourite bird is the Great Crested Grebe. It's great! The Romans called it *Podiceps cristastus*. It was almost extinct when Queen Victoria was the queen, but Aldous Huxley, writer of *Animal Farm*, raised a stink about women's hats. Feathers went out. I think the crest looks like a carpenter's pencil behind the ear, and they do build a nest like an ark. They are brilliant underwater swimmers. My gran says it's a wonder they don't catch polio.

Cormorants

They did not pass the test. Just past the school for private girls, in coats of strips of black blazers, they colonise the flooded pits.

Mallards

A delicate dad caught dabbling in Debbie Duck's drawer – a green glossy popsock caught at head and neck, lycra in chestnut for his chest, grey the rest. In the brown uniform of a money warden his chosen takes five ducklings through their mocks.

Heron

A greying Senior Lecturer in Fish Studies (Thames Valley), he stands in frozen hop concentration, regarding a lectern only he can see. Still, he gets results. He's hoping for a chair.

Swans

Pure snow: the remains of icebergs hauled from the Arctic Circle to cure a drought. Their beaks are municipal clamps.

Swan

A spotless aristocratic glove puppet. Its last song? Opera.

Cuckoo

It's an uplifting call and when you hear it spring is coming, sure enough, resurrection, promise kept. But I'm not comfortable. That's no life for her and it's no life for anyone else mixed up in the whole business. The parents think the chick is just like them, and it's a hero when it gets bigger. Then it's all me me me, eating its brothers out of home and house, breaking its foster-mother's heart as sure as. I can't speak to her about it, and she won't get help. She says: every one of my children is like a little Jesus, and that makes me... God.

Pigeons

Pedestrianise the High Street? Crumbs!

Song Thrush

Its shirt in ill-advised off-white, customised with blotches of crank-oil, a thrush prods the temporary car park. He/she almost forgets to repeat itself, but on a scaffold a song finds it and finds it again.

Ring Necked Parakeet

They call us Asians. I deny
nothing, neither grandad nor now.
It's just a collar. Please rely
on other data – know the how
beyond the costume green, the why
escaping when we sing our 'row',
the who our chokers signify:
a chain from chains, as times allow.

Carrion Crow

Headquarters could spare only a couple of officers, rheumatics in all-weather
macs. But the old boys knew what was what, they knew what wasn't.
Measuring the second field, not six metres from the wood's muddy edge,
they found the two of them. Four days, maybe five. 'A pact.'

Jay

We packed some snacks, cokes and beer, took the train out to Windsor and
walked up to the Great Park. It was September, but as you looked up the
avenue there was a heat haze at the knees of the giant Copper Horse and
Horseman. They looked like they were stepping out of the waves, turning,
about to bear down on you. 'Oaks this old always remind me of root ginger.'
We sat in a tree's shade on the tartan blanket he used to have in the car. A
stocky brightly coloured bird, chest pink as a perfume counter, flew down
from one of the other trees with an acorn in its beak. 'It's a Jay,' James said,
'Jay for Jane,' and then he was off, looking at me, laughing. We were both
smiling. 'J, the genesis of Joy, a Joint's full lips, first kiss of the spliff, fragrant
Jacaranda. Julep, Juju, too. Jay, trumpet-tumbled gentle Jericho, Japanese
pyJamas, ma Jolie Jeune fille, ma Joie de vivre, ma Je ne sais quoi.' 'J,' he
said, with an exaggerated sigh, 'my Jeopardy.' The bird had vanished by the
time he was finished that lot. He'd been doing actions. Later on, on the way
back into town, I saw another one, quite a way off, though he missed it.

Domestic geese

More woofers than tweeters, they guard Stereo Component with surround-sound.

Moorhen

They push and they push, and it seems to me they never reach the end of their beak – a stop button. And it's like they're made of delicate ashes themselves. Their first flight. Just to commemorate my two and think of them when I come out here.

Magpie

There are winners and there are losers in this life. You might as well be a winner. Motorway verges, council grounds, anything landscaped, fine. Have a recce, see what suits, move in. Some creature gives you a look, take its eyes out.

Kingfisher

Blue. I mean green. Blue, green.   Gone.

Lick and Stick

Lick and stick

For those who wish to experiment before committing themselves to an indelible design,
there is the temporary tattoo. This uses the 'lick-and-stick' method.

Staple's World of Body Art Website

It's a pleasure, this
　　lick-and-stick of something extinct, flexing,
　　　　　the dinosaur you backclassify a dragon,
　　　　　　　a far, long, cry
from the patch on your wrist,
bubblegum scented, a pirate, in orange and green,
a memory before you were ten
but you're fragrant now
as the print is moistened, firmed, as it's pressed
　　on the tension of your shoulder,
　　　　　smoothed for runkles,
　　　　　　　and now the graft unpeels
　　　　　　　　　skin from skin,
　　　　　　　　　　　　　no tearing this time,
　　　　　　　　　　　　no distortion, this time,
　　　　　　　　　　this
　　　　　　　　　　　time
'only the mouth
　　means more than the hide' –
as you say, you can't talk
　　　　　　　　in isolation,
in the shell of your skull
　　　　　　　the tongue's the sealife,
is more than surviving,
　　　　　　　　　　a little bright tongue
but your lips seem tender
　　– expecting a cold?
(this morning, I cut myself shaving,
feel your top lip, swollen)
so today no outré garish tawdry lippie
(the purple so dark it was all but black
in that fancydress bash in Islington –
through your gown your breasts like neat and
　　　　　　　　　　secret combinations,
　　　　　　　　　　　the door
　　　　　　　　　　　　of your four-square safe,

35

stroke sea anemones, unforgeable watermarks
                                        treasures in the cave –
got up in screens, an isotope technician, facemask and mitts,
and me, in much the same kit, a halfhearted impression
                        of a cardiac surgeon,
                                                a right pair
)
like the brackets your lips indent on your coverless pillow,
('the mouth,' I lisped, 'is half a kissh')
our parenthesis
                        chit chat
with your theories of flirting and surrogate skin
containing and hinting,
                                the article of clothing
                                                the definite article
more than a wraparound, life-time, one-off sentence –
you can't get away
                        with calling it clingfilm,
you can't dismiss selfgeneration –
delicate skirts (the leather veining
and veiling – re-vealing),
                                the point of gloves,
the emphasis of – switch – your lime pastiche of a cocktail dress,
your lipgloss, of fragrance, so often itself
from specialisation, sophistication, pungent beneath the flesh,
I mean identifier glands and their pheromones,
'furrymoans', speak in my defence, sipping liquid sugar,
and you own up publically
to threadworms descending, each night entwining
(remember that rave near Wraysbury?)
in the wee hairs of your arse, nibbling
at the dilatable membrane,
picked up, you'll be saying, fifty years on,
'from a squat, pun intended' – in Haringey
or a deb's comingout in Knightsbridge,
but the itch, you say, as if confidentially –
with mock nostalgia – was also an ache,
a yearning, a longing, like the sex of a purse still to be paid for,
your little moccasin with Fort Apache insignia,
and your telling admission, for a lover of serpents and markings,
that you were raised between Slough
        and (your snobbish embarrassment)
                                A Town Called Staines –

proclaimed you say by the Thames, the tattoo of the Thames,
a trumpet solo one side your spine, flowing the length
of your too-often tense back,
the Thames with the head of a snake,
optimistic and exotic, brilliant blue,

                                      'woad' you pipe up,
with all the royal houses and the palaces
of riverside stations, slipways and wharves,
their names and your birthdate, your epitaph (ominous space underlined)
                                          in calligraphy,
                                in words with edges,
and the river's free verse I have to insist
relying on pattern and the shape that contains it,
its flexible volume, its brimming, er-hm, genius
for composition (like the peach-, conch-like birthmark
                    the other side your verti-braes,
                                          facing
   the tidal reaches),
its genius for composition, for perspective and rubbish
like the breath that's got snagged
between m'mouth and ma lungs
as I wait on your lips, on your larynx, on your tongue,
the proof of telepathy, the uh-huh or nuht,
                                  the pleasure
of more than that show you swear you curated
of broch stones and bells from the first Chinese dynasty
and prostitutes' call cards from phonebooths in Bloomsbury,
Little Miss Delhi, 'Goa', Night Nurse and Rose,
with the kitsch of correction, of distraction, of
                                girls in their teens,
knickers from hospitals with x-rated xeroxes
of backsides and aprons –
an exhibition – an obsession –
                          with husks and small traces,
with scrapings and leavings, like the scratches in Orkney
of Vikings on holiday on the island prehistory urgently claims,
in that old cemetery, 'in this infirmary',
in postmodern games of quote
                        touching all but fertility,
leaving filaments to tease between juices,
                      to stretch
like rubber
   tapped from forests of delivering other' –

                              Christ, your Catholicism
rubs off quickly,
                      kicks in, I should say,
as unguents crack
                      the whip of the synapse,
and you've gone and come back
                              (shoulders, more carefully uncovered)
and won't be put down
as a leaver or lover, as no-ing or yes-ing,
of deciding a future, a rhythm or structure –
'You yourself aren't above it, beneath more like,
and no moral amoral artist scruples –
you'll be muttering freedom before you're quite finished –
something to do
                      with as close as possible
and still not knowing up to the minute, the whole shebang,
                                        the aphtha and swarfega,
with tasting just a layer, where underwear were, whatever wherever –'
like the perfume you'd expect a younger woman to wear
or barely scent, just the ghosts of shampoo
                                        squirt-measured this morning,
hair in the sink, darker for water,
but you're your father's daughter, adopted, just want to talk
                              critiques of dirt, of giving, of the body as art,
of what's gritty, what's earthy,
what's squalid, what's bitter,
what's evil, what's *what*,
(Doc Dwarf to Snow White –
'What are you,
                      and who are you doing?')
'what's it all worth' –
                              as I lie here beside you
in my skin and my name, in my dreams
(the ink is smudging,
no joke, the dragon's just smoke),
Rory Sangster v Terry Lean,
I mean
      who are you?, which much?
            I've always hardly known you,
will you
            be in touch?

Offices

Cleaners

The cleaners know

        the family photographs.

                Save and.

The system crashed

        accessing the account.

                Save and save and.

The air con died. I

        heard her voice.

                Save and save and save.

Save, and save, and save.

Save? / Send? / Delete?

You wouldn't know
not to know me.
Offices. Idle hope
in duplicates.

Takes
a no one
to know a someone.

*

(Is it she or her?,
since the you...
is talking to myself.)

*

It's absolutes,
like breathcatching nevers,
if I sing this.

*Is that a threat
or a premiss?*

*

No action required

and a bottle of red.
That was the original now:
mono before stereo.

'You.'

*

It's beautiful to have poise.

You... have poise.

*

Everything is brimming, and why
should you, should you believe
in in my arms? In my arms

like a tough song, actually,
with the know-how (in version 1.1
we're both a someone), which is not,
it's not being knowing, and just not sobbing
with the backing singers
at the overproduction and spliced duet.

'In my arms.'

It's attachment with audio
for company in this company,
totally out of it. Truly,
'truly, truly, truly' –
half appeal, half
highpitched promise –
all hope invested
in your hush hush
offshore trust.

*

Hush.

Trust?

As a

to say something – to say something – to

deferral
a pleasure
is it

good working relationship – thought we – a good

as a friend
as a colleague
as a friend

as a

in the red
actuary
that red

single figures – amounts – spoken for

do the sums

Marks & Sparks

Fishbones of aerials

An aerial: on a stick,
straight skeletons of fish.
A wok for the satellite dish,
nothing cooking.

A week past and counting
we tutted at the news, whatever,
ate together the hit-or-miss:

I talked myself to this,
out the recipe, the safe side
of the ledge.

I hear, like an empty fridge,
half rattle, half hum,
Eat the telecoms.

Kids

The window's open, the trees are fresh.
The kids know happiness
and they're kicking it between them.
I hope they hit our door.

I'd ask you for a game
but I've been told before.

Wasps

Autumn's here, the wasps
are trying to get in.

Home
is my crime too,
hope the sin.

Last spring you broke in,
took... everything.

Separate again

Come back to bed, forget the money.
When I said you needn't worry
I was thinking, 'separate again'.
Hear my sorry. Tell me when.

'Leave your keys by the mat:
we'll pick things up
after that.'

Wrong again

The taste of you
is strong on my tongue.
Let me go – I won't be long.
I'll get dressed and write the song
that tells our friends they were wrong.

You are
here for good?

Margin

Ache, braced against tremble.
I do want to, want to
see-you-for-the-third-time
again.

Surely a.

The fact was,
I'm on love with you,
darely.

One per cent
margin of horror.

'OK
I don't think.'

Holiday romance

All your everythings, no nevers
and more die-for-yous
than the
end of the limited offer.

Just fly.

A book and a bask.
You always take the time
to work me out,
hoist my flag.

For that
you can just sit back –
I'll always
open up to you.

Trust me,
I'm a...

deckchair.

Cadets

A bra's a parachute –
it was never going to open.

Listen, freefall
enfolds us.

We're lust and kindness.
Off comes

the undeveloped harness –
standard issue – released.

Above /
Beneath,

then

a tensing reach,
the stretch,
the duvet's net.

Touchdown.

Careless

I care for you.
You... could care less.

You cannot persuade
tenderness –

that's after hurt,
half-forgetting harm,

thinking you can know
a careless man.

Helpline

It's your life,
but I don't trust you with it.
You hark back to 'us',
I've lost track of it:
if that was love
you shouldn't... trade on it.

You've not been charged
for this call.

Twigs

Twigs mark my back in the Manor's wood,
twigs mark yours when we turn.
Taste of your mouth
and the smell of the wood,
heat of sweat returned.

Say you forget it now,
say you don't quite recall.
I know you're living it again,
I know you're seeing it all.

You're here with me in the Manor's wood,
you're here now – just like then.
'Over,' you say,
'It's over for good.
Nothing happens again.'

Tensioned frame

'Never,' by the pylon's feet
a mile from the village sign:
'Never,' you said,
and 'Only,' and 'Love,'

           and 'Mine.'

'Quiet,' in the electric field
beneath the tensioned frame.
'Quiet,' I said,
and 'Lonely,' and 'Love,'

           and 'Time.'

Less said

Though you left me
I worry about you.
Are you with someone
unsuitable?

The last time,
et cetera.

Sleep again, 'sleep' –
saying more then
than between
Kilmaurs and Kilbarchan,
the going good.
I was…

not as good as this.

Start again?
Find someone…

unsuitable?

Shoosh

Because
you were just like her,
she wasn't you.

Six years later, Sheila,
I remember your 'Shh',
our bodies
a greedy mouthful
on the hungry bed.

Today, your double's
unfashionable,
she wears your coat,
your conservative shoes...

When she looks,
'Shh,' I say to myself
without beginning your name.

I wish

'Let me down
in the bus bay?'

Hazard lights, idling,
wipers' tongues

dry, off. 'I,
I wish you well.'

'I wish *you* well.'

Actually holding hands.
'Friends?'

'You'll miss your.'
'I'll miss my.'

'I wish…
I wish.'

Passenger side

You flourish, alone.
For a second
even this face

could be a memory.
As yours is,
is so.

We both look back.
The car's the sound
of its own reversing,

suffered that quick
on the one way.
'The postbox is fine.

Promise you'll read?'

'Skirt'

Feet more delicate than yours
slant out from the duvet.
On the carpet a skirt
catches its breath;
that scent you avoid
pretends it's *déjà vu*.

My hands, I trust,
are not someone else's.

Behind you

I love you.

I'm nostalgic
for us and this table,
note the cups stacked up.

I said
nothing at work.

That painting behind you
is yours, a gift,
figurative and sensual
(open, even so, to abstraction).

The clock can't be read
on Assurance Buildings.

Remember instead
(rain tomorrow, too)
you were you,
we were us,
I was mine.

It was
British Summer Time.

Marks and Sparks

Of course I'm a novice,
meaning you're not?
I don't think so.

If it's not Marks and Spencer's,
product-tested,
what you're got up in
and how you're getting out it
still speaks volumes
(mail order,
or is it TV shopping?).

As you're anxious but asking
to open your shivering legs
I'll own up –
I'm out of myself
with nervous excitement,
hope I don't,
cough cough,
flood the two-stroke,

and I suppose your husband
fits like the proverbial
(my ex used to…).

Can I hurry you?

As, as

What falls between us
is the rain
as thick as, as fast as,

and you're there with your ornaments
and we're here with our tucked-up nets
(say the car-park dividing us joins us),

and the snow
is just heavier than leaves,
just more liquid,
plural as millions et cetera –
it's as fluid I mean
as creamy falling stars

and what falls between us
falls and finishes the.

'Bye,' I say, say,
and all of us, well, wave.

Then, again

Said so, didn't I? As the saying says, all
said and done, and done, well, not well, but finished,
over, good as, over and done to.

Holding but not gripping, a hold, holding out,
holding all that held us to, what's it called? Held,
you were held. How could you?

Deli

You're transparent – heart
in a twist of clingfilm,
lungs, flap flap flap.

Still fresh, those
other organs?
Talk about that?

(Behind the counter
your daughter's mother
offers you up.)

Fitted sheet

Now that we've untidied ourselves
kneel with me in our laps.
A kiss for our clothes' volcano –
that damp ash –
a kiss for that bing of slack.

On the puckered fitted sheet,
one alert, one asleep.

Engagement / Strike

After I happened
to know your label,
you container
for thing contained

we belonged
to our own bodies,
strikers maybe,

had, anyway,
to repeat ourselves,
a banner for our bed.

What that
explicit slogan said
is unreadable,
unread.

On, off, over

I love you,
and you,
and you

now sleeping, top on
from slipped off, finally,
over your shoulders,

now sleeping, not one
thought for me,
rightly,

now sleeping, right,
not a thought.
You were wrong.

I love you.

I bet

I don't know what I want

but she shouldn't say you're a tart,
I bet she likes it in the arse,
how much flesh
can you pierce
without whistling through your face,
a Japanese wind ornament?

I don't know what I want
but you shouldn't say she's prissy,
I bet sex is just birthdays
and Christmas
and no recognition
of the May Bank Holiday.

What do you want?

Odi et amo

You disgust me. I
love you. I.

Stop. asking. questions.
I.

Leave. me. alone.

Think for thinking

When can we be...
gentle again?

An eye-headache, car-noise.
We're wearing our foreheads,
offering... short tempers.

We're lessening

but the money and the space
and the money and the space

keep
on
promising.

Art lover

'Shh, you'll wake the baby,' –
first words
when you touch my fists,
tense in the dream.
No, I'm me.

Talk about romance
and you're just talking,
but your kiss,
your lips –

(Either way, I'm not bothered:
if we rise above ourselves
by being what we know we are
or by just denying it) –

you draw your hand
gently down my back,
a confident art-lover,
and you can have me
at almost your lowest bid.

A new establishment

A sudden weekend.

A friend fresh out of marriage
electrifies our entry-phone;
a backing-singer
pushed to a solo mike.

In our mucky hall
our parents' children's books
buzz like two-stroke engines.
One of us talks down.

When the storm door waives
man-made soles
flap breathily up the steps...

Later, our visitor in the close again,
the bracelet, the doorchain, is fast.
I unsaddle separates
from the bandy clothes-horse.

On the stereo
a single's black coffee
twirls its central cream.
Like a love-letter

we fold the bed-cover.

Scare

In a bin nothing ticks
and mats hair.

Are you in the concourse?
Your phone repeats openendedness

just for hours.

At supper here's us scoffing
eggs freckled in fat.

You're running the bath
like a recipe.

The radio-alarm is primed.

A hundred strokes
for your Long Player hair.

Lucky day

after Catullus

If anything yearned for, prayed for,
goes and happens
you've got to be grateful.

So I'm grateful – I'm richer than gold
now you're back,
all I yearned for.

Choose to come back, just like I wanted.
Come back, wanting to.

Sunlight. My lucky day.
Who in all the world
is happier?

What more
could you pray for
than this?

Call

I'm in love with you again
(privilege of elegy, binary of lyric)
and the mynahbird's unlearnt
the car alarm, moved up
to blackbird again, means it love.

You're the nightingale,
singing nightingale
(what's a nightingale
sing like?),

you're –
as if all this time sings up,
our time, our time again,
you, and I must admit,
me, answering back

As if

All your worries –
forget the lot
and hug me.

Hold's the word,
as if all's been said,
not yet done.

No, don't listen to me
religiously.
Just

know I'm yours –
if it's talk, if love.
If love, love.

Hand Held

for Katie

Angelman Syndrome is a neurological disorder caused by an abnormality in chromosome 15. Typically, sufferers have severe learning difficulties, problems walking and sleeping, epilepsy and no speech. They often have blonde hair, and usually have a happy disposition with frequent laughter.
Adapted from *Angelman Syndrome*, a leaflet produced by the Angelman Syndrome Support Group for parents and carers

A dash

When you were sick

all down a paperback
I'd grown up with at uni
we'd known a month
James/Kathleen was in our life.

The suits knew too
when *Mother*, work reports,
your purse and book
each need dished:
you'd just unclipped your case.

Your dash from Underground
to surface air, and then
(the bombs) no bins
in all the mall,
is just this tale, a joke,

but you were stranded, Jaq.

Lifer

All the world is in the ultrasound
– our lifer –
Scan-sat's cloudy picture,
the radiographer
reading your skin with a light-pen.

But no-go, belly for a blah-code,
until the kid gives in –
hands above her head.

And then that nose,
those in-di-vid-u-al toes,

and kick! kick! kick!
the miracle.

Than we are

Summer birds as small as leaves
and I'm calling it singing, that voluble tune.
The windows are open: it's mild and between
lackadaisical raining. Take it easy –
the car park's wrecks on bricks, cut grass.
The trees – aren't committed to the verb.

And here's our girl, four days for real –
and I'm calling it crying, that headache-making,
and will she sleep this time, and let *us* just sleep

and dream of her, better than we are
thirty years on.

Anne and the Royal

Was your father
a despatch rider
or just mentioned in despatches?

'You'd love the garden, Richard.
Flowers really grow in England.
Your dad's a softie, actually.
On Midsummer's Night
by Anne Hathaway's Cottage
he said: marry me.'

On Midsummer Night
in the Royal
you.

On Midsummer Night
in the Royal
you.

You'd love the garden, Mum,
or what it will be.
Flowers really grow in England,
honesty, thyme,
love-in-the-mist.

Jaq fixed a bath
and Kath had a splash
on the scrap of lawn.

Was your father
a despatch rider
or mentioned in despatches?

Flightpaths

Cormorants on the gravel pits,
gannets on a skerry.
Pelicans by the condo boards,
parakeets in Sydney?

More birds flew out
from the SS Pricey –
scuttled on a dryish patch
to start a family –
than those in a flap
in the old dove and raven story.

(The black and white telly
dreamed in colour,
a dream with a logo for a rainbow,
a charter,
and where's the remote?)

Back to the boat.
You could say Mrs Noah died,
and all her birds of paradise
got work in the colonies,
or thereabouts.
Noah, too.

Mum, and Dad, is that not you?
The ungainly creatures, migrated brothers?

'Keep closer, will you – promise me that.'

In each less and less makeshift flat
even the phone's a kind of bird.
Grip it by the head,
hold the chest and prod.
Connect what's left
of the flightpaths of the world.

Taps

Eight and hair like a girl's,
a wasp in my ear
in the garden scrub…
'snowberries'.

Twenty-eight, and it's worn
white porcelain, cool close up.
In the window of a shop
a girl kneads my hair.

Between taps
Mum firms my mop
(water, so brown locks
go black).

The wasp floats up.

Victory in Europe

Three, just past three,

almost asleep,
baby and Jaq, and me,
clean as a chart.

Ma, let's not part.
I'm a small father,
you an evacuee.

War over,
you'll ship back to start,
not mother me.

You'll not mother me.

'Speech absent'

A kiss, Katie
and you were gold.
As good as.

I think you know your name,
'Daddy' and 'Mummy',
not sure of 'home'.
Can't speak any.

Doctor Dad didn't know:
'What's a bad chromosome?'

Dopey has Angelman's Syndrome

Dopey has Angelman's,
keeps mum –
plays his days
with rubies,
all innocent fun.

Dopey's dopey –
the drugs he's on.

Dopey has Angelman's,
fits at night.
He's got Doc
and Happy
and Miss Snow White.

Thanks

Fractures, but mending
slowly, needs care,

and nothing forensic –
'dad', 'mum',
no crime tonight,

can't make the sign
of the remote

(so the sign
that's a hand on a shoulder,
the sign
of the eyes, of the mouth –
your eyes, your

mouth).

That's plenty,
plenty thanks.

Nothing promised

A bit dense at first maybe
didn't pick up
              your 'density'

                   ('substance
is the locus of, of qualities')

but sleepless for nothing promised,

to be honest, at first
you-in-your-clothes,
you-in-your-voice,

which isn't not a compliment either,

and then ideas together,
half-rhyming in bed,
a kiss is a rhyme

contains more
than its volume

(our little girl
balancing
between us,
almost standing,
holding

your right hand,
              my left hand,

the paper-chain).

So the palm faces

adapted from The Dictionary of British Sign Language / English

The left hand is held so the palm faces the signer,
the fingers pointing right.
The right hand is held palm facing the signer,
fingers pointing left.

The hands are held in front of the chest, at an angle
so the fingers are all turned up.
The back of the right hand is held
against the palm of the left.

The hands remain together
making a short movement towards the signer
so the right palm touches the chest.

affection

love

See, touch on the baby gym

a silver card cat
a fawn loofah
a pastel green-and-yellow teddy
    pull-toy in wood
a ladybird pull-toy in wood
    red and green and white and pink and black

a mackerel shield of fish holograms
a fawn stiff-bristle wooden-handled brush
a fawn flannel bag – inside
    a photo of Mummy in a blue and yellow tracksuit
    a starry navy silk ribbon
    a red red ribbon

a small basket the shape of a nest
a red snow flake / steamboat paddle that can spin
cold stainless steel bells the shape of plums
a plastic yellow bangle

two old cards –
>Christmas – the Nativity (straw and chubby angels)
>Congratulations on Your Wedding

Gallery / zoo

Katie reaches out
(speaking for myself
in the world of high art
I'm not that keen
on Cézanne),
but 'speech absent'

and the little boy
in the Inn at the Zoo
says, 'He's saying,
"Who's a pretty boy?"',
meaning the gargling
electronic cockatoo,
in the rafters,
above the ketchup.
'Who's a pretty boy?'

Receipt

Katie reaches out
all sticky fingers,
no tissues
(just cash, a poem)
and seeks my look
and laughs on receipt,
laugh beyond thinking,
and cannot say
and cannot say.

Little bear

Busy with a book
and *mah mah-mah*
mah-mah mah-mah
mah-mah mah-mah
mah-mah.

We've been told
of course this isn't
mother,

but picture of a bear
and you're a picture
Katie, called Ursula
in the short list,
little bear,
book on lap,
index finger
fixed, certain

but now you look up.

'That's right,' I chirp,
'It's Teddy.'

The clutter back

'It was Harry.'

Two days' stink
in the junk conservatory
(something your mother'd said,
'Cats are just animals.')

but half a soul
after all –
the hedgehog we'd fed
at the doorstep

fetid now
in Katie's nappy bin.

'I thought it was him.'
Your mum, almost laughing,
buried the thing,
scrubbed the trap.

We stacked the clutter back.
Before the light's
click,
you locked the glass door.

Abacus

Truth is, I
was ashamed.
I'd rather not say

on what count.
And a glance –
across our front room –

then I counted –
the total,
all our lifetime –

there, our daughter,
the fit subsided,
timed safe,

and –
'and' is a word for you –
you add up –

and I'm worse
than a bead of nothing.
Subtract

everything you could hope for.
Keep subtracting.

The grip

People will not love you
when we are dead.

A woman in a bib
saying nothing in screeches,
whose grip and spit and sleeplessness
lack all endearment,
though you have been
dear enough to us,
can only hope for what is yet
termed a home,

but it's some consolation
you understand nothing
of nuance, nor the future.

Only child

Pushchair,
now wheelchair,

pampers,
medical pants.

Each month,
you too, in a nappy.

The only child
not. too. happy.

bawls for noise,
for time,

for more of his kind.

Logger's Leap

An escalator underwater – just –
lugs the plastic dugout up.

The crew all slipped
from the same genetic dip –

number one trapper
is my brother's daughter,

all smiles, but a pliers-grip.
Her dad, captain of the ship

on his old polymer sledge,
is first at the high edge

of a frost-attacked
laminated cul de sac

half a life ago at least.
Katie, almost on her feet,

defies g and me –
as you see

I take a back seat
but must proceed

down the sluice
to photos of us.

R for Robert

In the Surrey hangar
veterans and rally drivers

re-wattle the Lancaster.
If you like, I'll demonstrate her.

Please,
the payload release.

The only monster
ever hawsered

out from the depths
of sullen Loch Ness,

this craft is a vast new cross;
resists a swastika's boss.

Slipping a hand –

              mine? –

                         on a Highland craftsy lane

                         Rob for Robert, not passed five,
                         explodes into his life.

                         A National coach bears down.
                         Everyone's a noun

                         save a single passer-by
                         lifting a kid these days

                         away from the target
                         of a headlight unit.

                         He is standing him,
                         safe as a bomb,

                         by a drum
                         for polishing gems.

blue, quilted

sand in the painting it's a shoreline
the woman in her husband's

flap flap yellow oilskins

the woman in remember Rob were you
too young to remember?

blue and quilted – Mum –

her old blue anorak, painting, am I
too old to remember?

(an empty beach, full of weather)

dark hair then grey hair
dark hair then grey hair

'all that time'

Mum Ma Mother

Eureka

Cool pale blue, warm,
plastic ceramic,
the mirrors steamed, surface
on a surface,
one third of a song
refraining, pouring and
patting the water, once, splish,
clothes in their
soft strata, layers on the lino,
time-that-was-around-you,
time now, settled,
dirt out – without clouding –
from the tiny-beaches-of-your-toes,
settling, washing that's a massage,
and the clear density of water
(substance-persists-through-tiredness),
in the pink, glowing through, oils
the thinnest of golden speckling
(the launch that's the lapping
molecules of bathwater
all moored by the plug –
heavy H's, the two of us,
chained to the stretched O,
renewable – or predators,
brightening in a lobster dinghy,
sinking/scalding) – the bath a low
tray for crafting an endpaper,
a terrine for a light soup,
a moulding for an ornamental pond

'Mmmmmmm.
Did you set the video?'

with fragrance, a scent
of palpable apricots,
your probably Spanish hair
wet at the fringes,
a new colour black that's delicate,
fused –

'Uh-huh.'

Fob

A smudge on the telly –
Katie's unwiped lick.
She's been mouthing
the slab of lens
while changing channels
(she thinks)
with the on/off.

'She thinks.'

Yes.

On the screen, a ball
not kicked for Scotland
furs –
for a good deal
less than a second.
It makes a fob
from the blear.

Then (you'd've taken in
that then), the ball sharpens –
quickens, veers.

Fifty thousand cheers!

It wins the World Cup.

The taps just flow hot and cold

Tonight, we dribble, we slur, we stutter –
mumbler Price, and his priceless daughter, the spit.
Mute? Don't mention it – we hardly ever.
We just mutter and gasp, and laugh –
Katie's singing when she's bah-ing in the bath,
and we are champions of grin, champions of lisp.
We are champions – of the trembling lip.

Let's dry yourself now.

Here.

For Katie's toes

One's a rat
nosing all the bins.
Two's a goose
laughing on the wing.

Three's a pig
grinning with a squeal.
Four's a mouse
trembling in the field.

Five –
if you catch him alive –
undoes locks…

He's a hungry fox!

The world is busy, Katie

The world is busy, Katie, and tonight
the planes are playing, fine, alright, but soon
the folk behind those blinks will nap, sleep tight,
as you will too, beneath a nitelite moon.
The world is busy, Katie, but it's late –
the trains are packing up, the drunks are calm.
The fast, the slow, has gone. It's only freight
that storms the garage lane. It means no harm.
The world is busy, Katie, but it's dark –
the lorries nod, they snort, they spoil their chrome.
They hate to be alone. For them, a lay-by's home.
The world is busy, Katie, like I said,
but *you're* the world – and tired. It's time for bed.

The late show

Tonight, lashings of crime,
wisecracks and crisps.
'Lager, please. You?'

A yell –

our insomniac
faking a snake
spotted in the cot
not yawning.

Ten seconds and she's biting
like an angel,

laughing in my arms,
demanding, maybe,
the story of Noisy
(ducks are good, too),
cats at tricky angles…

Words – hands –
come first (the alphabet
on hold), then food.

'Katarina,
fancy a pizza?'

Air miles

This crate has flown a world or two.
Fatigue's in the craft – it's in the crew.
We're case-hardened, brittle.
Cracks mark the metal.

That song

What replaces prayer? –
since I can't, now,
honestly pray.

To be honest
I don't believe,
but trust in trust today.

She chose me then.

She chooses me again.

Wake up and play

Wake up and play
dot-to-dot with the stars.
I can see a horse,
and a yacht, and five sports cars.

Your old red purse
is up there, too,
with your college bike
and one court shoe.

Look at the riches: rings
and phantom gold bars.
Wake up and play
dot-to-dot with the stars.

Time thieves softly,
faster than fast.
You can't keep up
with the speed of the past...

The sky is so bright –
the clearest so far.
Wake up and play
dot-to-dot with the stars.

Sleeper

The stars finish with you –
you'll not wake up
for a comet or the moon,
or the shouts on overtime –
you're the sleeper
the crew out the back won't budge,
hammering by lights on sticks,
inching the tracks
back to true.

Poem's ending to do.

You –
are finished with the stars
but your daughter, starting, starts you.

The price–dream ratio

That day, futures doctors
couldn't locate
the trembling market's heartbeat.

lastminute.com…
                    steadied some
an infancy later.
You were crouched in labour,
showing the ward's drugs
and technofever
that defiant arse.

Just – one – last –
chance.

Our portfolio
                    bet near all
on the price–dream ratio,
a daughter or a son,
and in 'just' nine cricked months
(say sickness, say sciatica,
and that's for short), was

finally
paying
out.

'Ellen.'

Surely the certainties

surely the certainties
ach and ash
surely the certainties

baby talk
practising...
everything

(words for / sounds of /
sounds –
of sounds)

surely the certainties
ach and ash
surely the certainties

(   )

just ask

Fast

The stitches do dissolve, the skin the youngest, fast
to half a life, to murmur tender first, our life

refrain from just exact repeats, repeats the soft,
a voice, the used to voices, sure, assured,

beyond the fast, the suture last observed, released,
the loss allowed, the loss outlived, as if

the past need not arrest us, tag detached, alert,
past curing, all despair detained, the future else.

The sob is not the boss. The sob is not the boss.

The sob

is not

the boss.

'I have two daughters'

I have two daughters –
a manatee and a mermaid –
a mermaid, a manatee –
precious sea creatures.

The twins

This morning (some deer
always bear twins)
here's two foxes –
blethering, quite the thing –
a blink past a station
not safe to name.

It's playtime: Katie,
seven and a half,
takes her first judged steps –
sixty, her teacher has assessed
(she makes no sense),
but thirty at least
the girls in Woolworths verify.

0 to 60
in seven and a half years.

Standing room only. Tonight,
in their redless suits
the foxes sweat, are overdressed.
It's the heat, the trackside dust.
Each and every beast
is just… way too hot to chew the fat.

Ellen sounds 'duck' for everything.
She leads her elder sister
round the rounded furniture.
She's a chubby hunter
saving… the last European bear.

A bow-tie pattern

My daughter's defiance just now
– the momentum of sobbing –
just because it was bedtime.

Lovely Ellen.

I remember my own tears
and a bow-tie pattern,
the tense crossed wires
of bedsprings above me
(I was lying an inch
from Dad's angry reach),
and my raw-throated sobs

when the woman I always knew
was wrong for me, finally left –
and I was relieved, and desolate.

Please

Oh.
Come here, come here.
Come on.
I know. I know.
Shoosh love.
Shoosh now.

It's OK. It's OK.
Everything,
everything is alright.
Come on now.
Sweetheart,
please.

Dad!

Speak!

Speak, Dad.

I can do a twenty-piece puzzle.

Dad!

Dad?

Hand held

No smile, smiler, blink and camera-shake.
A top's neck of milksoak and talc smell, Katie,
and babyskin's and spit's: bits of this-that's-you
(push-crashed into then then, but now
and holding), hands as loved as hands, hand!,

and

whatever your clear eyes are meaning
you mean it brightly.

A News

A news

I'm low, and the news
has purchase.

That's nothing.

I've said nothing
for years:

the life of a child,
hear-tell

a plague.

You are
so generous

with your silence.

You.

(I have news. Is it
news?

Good news?)

The truants will be suspended

School children walk out –
against the war. It's a war

against janitors. 'He
minded empty government

empty government buildings.
My father

was in there.' Smart,
the kids are smart –

they see us, precisely.

An authority

for the hostages at Camp X-Ray

A kind
of authority.

Infantry
taken as generals,
blindfolded.

Pleas, and no
civil answers.

(The one
tender meeting

is a crisscross,
tensioned wires

in the holding mesh.)

Deportment / Deportation

A plane with a bump on its head
lowers its clutch of wheels
and the test is over
for the hypothermic stowaway.

He turns up, early for work,
an impact on the car park
of Commercial Voice and Data.

His brother
survives the amateur cryogenics,
an IOU for A&E,
refugee remand.

Just one last trip
on the world's favourite airline
then –

securely home.

Slow films

A conversation

over a few days,
that conversation

in three hours.

Starting to know
people.

What happened?

Softened, bright

Computer light improves any painting,
back-lit for a radiant show.
Vermeer's balance, even,
glistenises, remains in its glisten.

The casual folds – those drapes –
stay, too, but know fabric now
as memories can think they know
what was best, what was
likely true.

Back-lit for a virtual exhibition:
I haven't a single picture of you
(days that did know what a day was),
can't now.

Softened, bright.

It's so good to have the,
to have the technology.

Big Bang research

I know them by their poems,
attachments that can't be read.

'It's just finished. Not really. Is that
last line way too much?'

Then I'm tap tapping,
saying, 'Visits

are my favourite poems.
Come and stay... the week?'

Letters arrive, less.
Could paper be made from leaves?

Autumn's over. We're binary
but we're not just digits –

I hear attachments, attachments
were an accident

of Big Bang research.
The upgrade (you know

this new upgrade?) –
the upgrade

will read everything.

All Light

All light

All light, even, is bundled
back into that black hole,
calibrated by darkness, by
density's ideal.

Energy, as well, can't resist –
forgets the struggle,
gathers presence before oblivion in a high style.
How can what be known?

It's all one to me, all of them, and the past –
jealous of the helpless,
kissed and crushed,
laid summarily to rest – that's the future, with no fuss.

'More mutters on dark matter.'

No one sees inconsequence like a stargazer,
or knows nothing so well.
'Park that radio dish somewhere else, can't you?'

Questions, questions.

Remind me what planet you've earned, what year this was going to be?
Security is just tomorrow's ifs and buts
tallied against community,
untold loss with a cartoon sigh and a mope,
velocities of near-love.

When? When? When?

Xerox me *Gravity Simplified* when you've solved that one. No –
you can send instead an *A–Z* of the unknown universe.
Zero-worship – nothing's better.

In your generous hours

In the plantation of focus-grouped trees, allow the pine-marten,
    the bumbling mourning simple capercaillie,
    the cross-bill's *glip-glip*,
allow the lips, the licks
             of sea-lochs,
    the dribbling pouts of dams,
allow the crime
    of the bramble, the nettle's spite,
give the light some latitude, snagging in your lungs
(the coughers have coffers, the kissed their kist),
allow to exist
    the ledge, as a place of flowers,
allow, in your generous hours, by the
    substantiated cities,
    the suburbs, their off-the-hanger song,
    their greed to belong, to pretend to the lens and breath of the country,
be friendly
    in dialects of body language telepathy,
assume trust
    with credulous fish, with defactoried cattle,
allow a little attar at the altar,
stay confidential with your future
    to the limits of scanners
    (wipe the screen's bleary plate),
you better not be late
    for enjoying the making of things –
make things
    (includes silence –

)
you have a licence to treasure affection in the diving chamber,
    to welcome, partner, from our recovery slumber,
        our plural known as 'lovers',
to discover
    the places that happened to grow you up in,
        the schools and the schemes,
        the smokes and the smacks,
oh, you better relax,
you're attached to the universe
    by the tenderest of chances:
make allowances.

Allow me.

Farewell remembering a goodbye

after César Vallejo

In the end, finally, the finish,
turning, revolved and ended and moaning for you, giving you
the key, my hat, this little note for everyone.
At the end of the key the metal so we understand
how to ungild the gold, and in the end
of my hat, this poor, badly combed brain,
and there (a last glass of smoke, play-acting)
this soul's practical dream rests.

Goodbye, brother saint peters,
heraclituses, erasmuses, spinozas!
Goodbye, pathetic bolshevik bishops!
Goodbye, provosts in chaos!
Goodbye, wine that's in water like wine!
Goodbye, alcohol that's in the flood.

Goodbye, as well, I say to myself,
goodbye, formal flight of milligrams!
Goodbye, as well, in the same way,
chill of the chill and chill of the warmth!
In the end, finally, the finish, the logic,
the limits of fire,
the fare-thee-well remembering this goodbye.